IRWIN

QUICK START MASTERS

TECHNOLOGY

SOC
AND FINE ART
LEVEL A
Grades 1-2

Project Coordinator and Contributor: Ruth Brandon

Contributors: Lydia Cartlidge, Gary Gibson, Marilyn L. Legault, Claudette Sims, Elizabeth Verrall, Giselle Whyte

Reproducible Activities
Using Classroom Technology

Cover and title page art: Paul Wiersma
Cover Design: Donna Guilfoyle/ArtPlus Limited
Interior Design: ArtPlus Limited
Page Makeup: Leanne Knox/ArtPlus Limited
Edited by: Jeff Siamon

1 2 3 4 5 01 00 99 98 97 96
Printed in Canada

Published by
Irwin Publishing
1800 Steeles Avenue West
Concord, ON L4K 2P3

Contents

Introduction

Looking at Technology

Technology, part of Irwin Publishing's elementary reproducible activity masters series *Quick Starts*, is a series of activity-based books that bring technology into the classroom. Use them with your students as stand-alone lessons or as a starting point from which to integrate the use of technology with curriculum. These activities have been designed by teachers (and classroom tested!) to provide problem-solving approaches to common themes and subject areas. Here, students will find a variety of interesting and self-motivating things to do that can accommodate their various learning styles and developmental stages. Many activities are in an open format.

But *Technology* is not a study course in technology in itself. Rather, it challenges students to use technology as a *tool* in achieving their learning objectives. This distinction is important. Just as mathematics can be studied as a subject in itself, so it also can be employed to solve problems in other subject areas. Similarly, technology in the classroom is able to extend students' problem-solving abilities. In an increasingly complex and changing world, it is essential that students acquire the knowledge, skills, and strategies that will help them function. Understanding and using technology is an important part of this acquisition.

You might want, however, to explore with your students the broader concept of technology (if you haven't already done so). Certainly, it can be a much misunderstood term—not just electronics and computers. The ancient Egyptians employed technology to build the pyramids long before the first microchip. So while students will use many "state-of-the-art" devices, they will also utilize ordinary cameras, overhead projectors, common tools (probably the oldest form of technology), and other mechanical and electrical apparatuses.

Looking at Contents

Each book in the *Technology* series includes twenty-eight theme-based activities in one of the following curriculum areas:
- Social Studies and Fine Art,
- Science and Technology,
- Language Arts,
- Mathematics.

There are three achievement levels and books for each of the above subjects:
- Level A—Grades 1 and 2,
- Level B—Grades 3 and 4,
- Level C—Grades 5 and 6.

Of course, these levels can be adapted to suit the learning abilities of your students.

A teacher resource page is on the back of each reproducible student activity sheet. Each activity is identified by a Title, Theme, and Subject, as well as by a graphic that represents the theme. (The same graphic is on both the teacher and student pages.) Also identified on the teacher resource page are the activity's Materials list, Learning Outcomes, Inquiry/Thinking Skills, and Learning Strategies. The latter information might be especially useful when creating tracking and evaluation forms.

Icons on the bottom of each activity page indicate which technologies will be used. (See inside front cover for a complete list.) As well, suggestions for activity groupings are shown.

Three matrixes have been included for your convenience:
- theme and technology matrixes for this book,
- subject theme matrix for all the books in this curriculum area.

Looking at Social Studies and Fine Art, Levels A, B, and C

The Social Studies and Fine Art *Technology* books embrace a broad range of topics. The Social Studies component includes:

- environmental studies,
- relationships with family and society,
- past and present ways of life at home and abroad,
- world geography.

Whether using CD-ROMs, video cameras, computer modems, or other forms of technology, students will be motivated to gather, store, process, and communicate information. In addition, because of the constantly increasing wealth of print and visual material, they need to have the necessary skills to be able to access, analyse, and interpret this information. Through the use of the various technological resources available, students will be able to take a more meaningful look at their own and other cultures, which hopefully will lead to increased understanding and social responsibility.

The Fine Art component incorporates technology into drama, visual arts, and music. Through practical, hands-on activities, students explore these disciplines using the equipment and tools that are part of their everyday lives. They are encouraged to develop creative skills for personal expression and communication that can be carried on beyond the classroom.

Theme Matrix
Social Studies and Fine Art, Level A

Theme	Title	Groupings*	Technology
Celebrations	4/Birthdays (FA)	Individual; Class	
	12/Making Greeting Cards (FA)	Pairs; Groups	
Communication	6/Dial 911 (SS)	Individual; Pairs; Class	
	23/Talking with Others (SS)	Individual; Pairs; Groups; Class	
Countries	7/Folktales (SS)	Individual; Class	
Family	3/Before and After (FA)	Individual; Groups	
Feelings	22/Smile! (FA)	Pairs; Groups	
Food	20/Sharing Apples (SS)	Individual; Class	
Games	26/Toy Groups (SS)	Groups; Class	
Geography	13/Map Making (SS)	Individual; Class	
Inventions	9/I'm a Robot, Too! (FA)	Individual; Groups; Class	
	10/Looking at Machines (SS)	Individual; Groups	
Jobs	19/School Helpers (SS)	Pairs; Class	
	28/Work Tools (SS)	Individual; Pairs	
Mapping	1/A School Tour (SS)	Groups; Class	
Monsters	15/Movie Monsters (FA)	Individual; Groups; Class	
Oceans	18/Ocean Life (SS)	Individual; Pairs	
People	8/Friends (SS)	Pairs	
Pets	11/Lost Dog! (FA)	Individual; Class	
Rain Forests	5/Computer Art (FA)	Individual	
Shapes	16/My New Classroom (FA)	Individual; Class	
	27/Two Ways of Looking (FA)	Individual; Groups	
Tools	14/More Tools (SS)	Individual; Groups; Class	
	24/Telephone Calls (SS)	Groups; Class	
	25/Tools We Use (SS)	Individual; Groups; Class	
Transportation	2/Airplane, Boats, Cars, and Trains (SS)	Individual; Groups; Class	
	17/Name That Sound! (SS)	Individual; Pairs; Class	
	21/Sing a Song (FA)	Pairs; Groups; Class	

*Groupings: • = Individual; •• = Pairs; ⁙ = Groups; ⁙ = Class

SS = Social Studies, FA = Fine Art

Technology Matrix
Social Studies and Fine Art, Level A

Technology	Title	Theme	Groupings*
(cassette)	9/I'm a Robot, Too! (FA)	Inventions	Individual, Groups, Class
	11/Lost Dog! (FA)	Pets	Individual, Class
	23/Talking with Others (SS)	Communication	Individual, Pairs, Groups, Class
(books)	18/Ocean Life (SS)	Oceans	Individual, Pairs
	23/Talking with Others (SS)	Communication	Individual, Pairs, Groups, Class
(paintbrush)	3/Before and After (FA)	Family	Individual, Groups
	7/Folktales (SS)	Countries	Individual, Class
	8/Friends (SS)	People	Pairs
	13/Map Making (SS)	Geography	Individual, Class
	14/More Tools (SS)	Tools	Individual, Groups, Class
	15/Movie Monsters (FA)	Monsters	Individual, Groups, Class
	16/My New Classroom (FA)	Shapes	Individual, Class
	19/School Helpers (SS)	Jobs	Pairs, Class
(lego)	16/My New Classroom (FA)	Shapes	Individual, Class
	27/Two Ways of Looking (FA)	Shapes	Individual, Groups
(camera)	3/Before and After (FA)	Family	Individual, Groups
	4/Birthdays (FA)	Celebrations	Individual, Class
	8/Friends (SS)	People	Pairs
	12/Making Greeting Cards (FA)	Celebrations	Pairs, Groups
	22/Smile! (FA)	Feelings	Pairs, Groups
	27/Two Ways of Looking (FA)	Shapes	Individual, Groups
(CD)	2/Airplanes, Boats, Cars, and Trains (SS)	Transportation	Individual, Groups, Class
	7/Folktales (SS)	Countries	Individual, Class
	8/Friends (SS)	People	Pairs
	14/More Tools (SS)	Tools	Individual, Groups, Class
	18/Ocean Life (SS)	Oceans	Individual, Pairs
	23/Talking with Others (SS)	Communication	Individual, Pairs, Groups, Class
(laptop)	5/Computer Art (FA)	Rain Forests	Individual
	11/Lost Dog! (FA)	Pets	Individual, Class

*Groupings: • = Individual; •• = Pairs; ⠒ = Groups; ⠿ = Class
SS = Social Studies, FA = Fine Art

Technology Matrix
Social Studies and Fine Art, Level A

Technology	Title	Theme	Individual	Pairs	Groups	Class
(laptop)	12/Making Greeting Cards (FA)	Celebrations		••	••	
	13/Map Making (SS)	Geography	•			••
	17/Name That Sound! (SS)	Transportation	•	••		••
	18/Ocean Life (SS)	Oceans	•	••		
	19/School Helpers (SS)	Jobs		••		••
	21/Sing a Song (FA)	Transportation		••	••	••
	23/Talking with Others (SS)	Communication	•	••	••	••
	28/Work Tools (SS)	Jobs	•	••		
(mouse)	1/A School Tour (SS)	Mapping			••	••
	6/Dial 911 (SS)	Communication	•	••		••
	15/Movie Monsters (FA)	Monsters	•		••	••
	17/Name That Sound! (SS)	Transportation	•	••		••
	19/School Helpers (SS)	Jobs		••		••
	21/Sing a Song (FA)	Transportation		••	••	••
	23/Talking with Others (SS)	Communication	•	••	••	••
	25/Tools We Use (SS)	Tools	•		••	••
(microwave)	20/Sharing Apples (SS)	Food	•			••
(overhead projector)	19/School Helpers (SS)	Jobs		••		••
	27/Two Ways of Looking (FA)	Shapes	•	••		
(movie camera)	8/Friends (SS)	People		••		
	11/Lost Dog! (FA)	Pets	•			••
(telephone)	6/Dial 911 (SS)	Communication	•	••		••
	24/Telephone Calls (SS)	Tools			••	••
	25/Tools We Use (SS)	Tools	•		••	••
(drill)	10/Looking at Machines (SS)	Inventions	•	••		
	14/More Tools (SS)	Tools	•		••	••
	24/Telephone Calls (SS)	Tools			••	••
(sander)	15/Movie Monsters (FA)	Monsters	•		••	••
	23/Talking with Others (SS)	Communication	•	••	••	••

* Groupings: • = Individual; •• = Pairs; ⁝ = Groups; ⁛ = Class;

SS = Social Studies, FA = Fine Art

A School Tour

Name _____

Members of my group: _____

1. Three places to go on our tour:
(a) _____ (b) _____ (c) _____

2. This is how to get from the classroom to place a:

- _____
- _____
- _____

3. This is how to get from place a to b:

- _____
- _____
- _____

4. This is how to get from place b to place c:

- _____
- _____
- _____

5. This is how to get from place c to the classroom:

- _____
- _____
- _____

6. Give your tape to another group to test.

IRWIN
QUICK START MASTERS

Title: **A School Tour**

Theme: **Mapping**

Subject: **Social Studies**

Materials Needed: Tape recorders.

Learning Outcomes:
• Describe orally the location of key areas within the school.
• Use simple directions.

Inquiry/Thinking Skills: Application and comprehension.

Learning Strategies: Organizing.

TEACHING STRATEGIES

1. Go on a walking tour of the school to locate and observe key areas (office, library, gym, first aid, washrooms, etc.).

2. Discuss with students why it is important for people to know the location of these places.

3. Divide students into groups. Tell them that each group will record a tour of the school. Allow each group member to tape-record one part of the tour.

4. Demonstrate the correct use of the tape recorder. Remind students to turn off the tape recorder between messages in order to allow the listener travelling time.

5. Brainstorm the types of information and directional language needed to be included on the tapes: *walk forward, turn right, turn left, return the same way, go past three doors, walk upstairs, etc.*

6. Finished tapes may be exchanged with other groups to be tested.

SOMETHING TO THINK ABOUT

▶ Ask students to draw a map of the school after listening to a tape from another group.

Airplanes, Boats, Cars, and Trains

Name _____

1. How do you go places? Do you go by car? by bus? by airplane? by train?

2. Find pictures on a CD-ROM that show how people go on trips.

3. Print out the pictures.

4. Look at all your pictures. Talk about ways you can group them. Pick a name for each group.

   ▶ **Where they go:** Land, Water, Air
   ▶ **People that ride:** 1 person, 2 to 8 people, 9 to 60 people, more than 60 people

5. What group do you like best? Why?

   _____

   _____

Title:	**Airplanes, Boats, Cars, and Trains**
Theme:	**Transportation**
Subject:	**Social Studies**

Materials Needed: Any CD-ROM program that has pictures of different modes of transportation.

Learning Outcomes: •Be able to classify objects.

Inquiry/Thinking Skills: Comprehension and analysis.

Learning Strategies: Comparing and observing.

TEACHING STRATEGIES

1. Discuss how objects can be classified in more than one way. You can use the students' shoes or any other suitable objects:
   - shoes that are white,
   - shoes that are laced,
   - shoes that are old,
   - shoes that boys or girls wear.

   Practise giving titles to the groupings. You may want to use hoops to make Venn diagrams.

2. Demonstrate how to find pictures with a CD-ROM encyclopedia that has different modes of transportation. Show students how to print out the pictures.

3. Have students print out pictures and classify them in different ways. (See activity sheet.)

SOMETHING TO THINK ABOUT

▶ Invite students to observe vehicles in their neighbourhood and classify them. These can be graphed according to colour, kind, etc.

Before and After

Name_____

1. What were they doing <u>before</u> and <u>after</u> the photograph?

2. Take a photograph of your friends.

3. Draw two pictures the same size as your photograph. Show what happened:
- before the photograph,
- after the photograph.

4. Glue your pictures like this:

(a)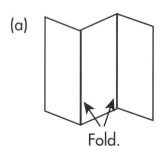
Fold.

(b)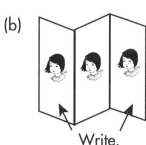
Write.

Title: **Before and After**

Theme: **Family**

Subject: **Fine Art**

Materials Needed: Polaroid camera, film, cardboard paper, pencil crayons or markers.

Learning Outcomes:
• Construct a photograph with purpose.
• Operate a Polaroid camera.

Inquiry/Thinking Skills: Analysis, application, and synthesis.

Learning Strategies: Constructing, illustrating, and sequencing.

TEACHING STRATEGIES

1. Instruct students on the proper use and care of a Polaroid camera.

2. Using sample photographs from the school or magazines, discuss with the students the temporal nature of photographs: they illustrate only one moment in time. Have students examine the samples. Ask them to describe what happened *before* or *after* the events in the photographs. Discuss with them some of these possibilities.

3. Request that students complete their activity sheets:

• Have students use a Polaroid camera to take an action photograph of classmates.

• Ask them to draw two pictures the same size as their photographs. Picture one will show what was happening before their photograph was taken. Picture two will show what was happening after the photographed moment.

• Tell them to fold a piece of cardboard into thirds and mount the three pictures in order. Display the pictures around the classroom.

SOMETHING TO THINK ABOUT

▶ Challenge students to plan and photograph a series of sequential pictures to illustrate an event. Ask them to work in groups where each student shoots and adds a caption to one photograph. Plan one photograph for each person in the group to show how to do something (how to operate a computer, how to make a telephone call, how to bake a cake, etc.).

Birthdays

Name _____

1. Every year you have a birthday. What do you do? What do your friends do on their birthdays?

2. What I do on my birthday: _____
   _____
   _____

3. This is what my friend _____ does on _____ birthday:
   _____
   _____
   _____

4. Make a birthday timeline. It can look like this:

1	2	3	4	NOW
Your baby photo	Your first steps photo	A family photo when you were three	A photo of you riding your bike	Your last birthday photo

5. Ask someone to take your birthday picture. Put your birthday picture on your timeline.

6. Show your timeline to a friend.

IRWIN
Q
QUICK START MASTERS

Title: **Birthdays**

Theme: **Celebrations**

Subject: **Fine Art**

Materials Needed: Polaroid camera, personal photographs.

Learning Outcomes:
- Describe ways in which birthday celebrations are observed by themselves and others.
- Communicate similarities and differences of birthday celebrations through photographs.

Inquiry/Thinking Skills: Analysis, application, and synthesis.

Learning Strategies: Recording, sequencing, and viewing.

TEACHING STRATEGIES

1. Through discussion, draw out the similarities and differences among birthday celebrations held by students in the class. Depending on the composition of the class, various ethnocultural and religious backgrounds may influence these celebrations.

2. In co-operation with home, have students bring to school photographs representing past birthdays. Tell them they are going to make a Birthday Timeline. Ask students to sequence their photographs like the example on their activity sheet. The photograph for the present year may be taken at home or at school with the classroom Polaroid camera. (Prior to the students using the camera for this photograph, review the handling and safety rules.)

3. As the timelines are completed, encourage students to examine the photographs for similarities and differences among the students. Challenge them to look beyond the people in the photographs. In another discussion, ask students to comment on the quality of the recent Polaroid photographs and how they may be improved if necessary.

SOMETHING TO THINK ABOUT

▶ Encourage students to draw a picture and write a story about next year's birthday. You can extend this activity further with the students writing captions for the photographs or writing a paragraph about the changes represented in their timelines.

Computer Art

Name _____

1. Make a rain-forest picture. Use a computer drawing program.

2. What will you put in your picture?

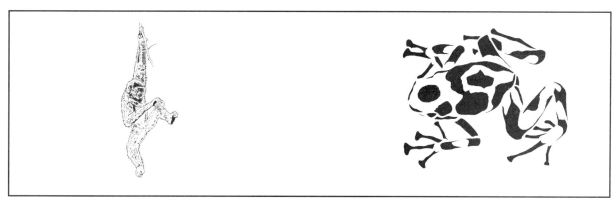

monkeys   **frog**

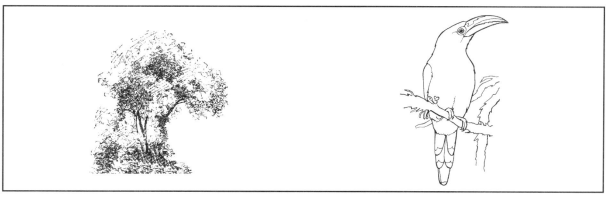

trees   **bird**

3. Print out your picture in colour, or colour your black-and-white picture.

Title:	**Computer Art**
Theme:	**Rain Forests**
Subject:	**Fine Art**

Materials Needed: Primary graphics or drawing software, computer.

Learning Outcomes: • Use appropriate terms to design ideas and techniques in their own works of art.

Inquiry/Thinking Skills: Application, comprehension, knowledge, and synthesis.

Learning Strategies: Creating, designing, and using.

TEACHING STRATEGIES

1. Talk about the rain forest with students. Discuss with them what and where it is. You might want to show them a video or selected picture books.

2. Tell them they are going to make a rain-forest picture to show others what the rain forest is like. They are also going to use a computer to create the illustration.

3. Many art programs have clip art that relates to the rain forest. Have students use and modify this clip art to make their illustration. Encourage them to use the other art options to create their own rain-forest environment.

4. Ask them to print out their pictures in colour if possible. Otherwise, have them consider using textured fills when printing in black and white.

Dial 911

Name _____

1. Why would you dial 911?

2. What help would you need?

Title: **Dial 911**

Theme: **Communication**

Subject: **Social Studies**

Materials Needed: Toy or real telephones, chart listing the emergency number (911) along with the help that this emergency number could provide (fire, police, ambulance, etc.), telephone directory, tape recorder and microphone (if needed).

Learning Outcomes: • Follow safety rules and describe ways to obtain emergency help.

Inquiry/Thinking Skills: Analysis, evaluation, and synthesis.

Learning Strategies: Discussing, problem-solving, and role-playing.

TEACHING STRATEGIES

1. Discuss the significance of the 911 number and outline its use as highlighted in the local telephone directory.

2. Have students present a number of scenarios that would constitute an emergency requiring 911 help. Ask them to illustrate on their activity sheets one of these events and the help that would come.

3. List with students the essential kinds of information that a 911 call must include. Discuss why each is important.

4. Have a pair of students role-play a call to 911 to illustrate the necessary social and safety skills involved. Encourage the students to comment on the role play, focusing on the information provided to the 911 source and on general telephone manners. Challenge them to practise 911 emergency calls using a variety of situations. Tape-record their skits. Evaluate these dramatizations with the class, listening for good safety practices and proper telephone etiquette.

SOMETHING TO THINK ABOUT

▶ These role-play situations could also be videotaped for further evaluation.

Folktales

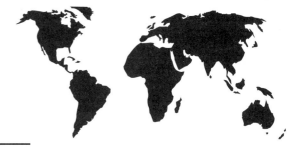

Name_____

1.   This is the name of the folktale book:

   _____

2.   The author's name is _____

3.   Here is the part of the story I liked best:

Draw a picture.

IRWIN
QUICK START MASTERS

Title: **Folktales**

Theme: **Countries**

Subject: **Social Studies**

Materials Needed:	Folktale storybooks from around the world, computer, electronic atlas or encyclopedia, poster board, drawing materials.
Learning Outcomes:	• Gather information from an electronic source. • Display information in an attractive way using cutting and pasting.
Inquiry/Thinking Skills:	Application, comprehension, knowledge, and synthesis.
Learning Strategies:	Displaying, identifying, researching, and writing.

TEACHING STRATEGIES

1. Read a folktale storybook from a country of one of your students. (You might also want to make this a library day where students, with the help of the librarian, find folktale books from around the world.) Help students record the title and the author's name on their activity sheets.

2. Use an electronic atlas or encyclopedia to find the country of the folktale. Have students print out a country map. Help them find other pictures that show its climate, the principal cities, the style of dress, and other interesting information.

3. Ask students to print out three screens they find interesting and informative. Tell them to use these screens, the map, and their own drawing to make a folktale poster display.

4. Share these posters with the rest of the class.

Friends

Name_____

Name of Friend	Special Interests	Skills	Why I Like My Friend

IRWIN
QUICK START MASTERS

Title: **Friends**

Theme: **People**

Subject: **Social Studies**

Materials Needed: Filmstrip projector, tape recorder, video digitized image, tape, glue, pencils, coloured bristol board, stories on filmstrips, and CD-ROMs.

Learning Outcomes:
- Use various types of information technology for a variety of purposes within and outside the school.
- Identify and demonstrate respect for the rights, skills, and interests of others.
- Use social skills in small-group work.

Inquiry/Thinking Skills: Application, comprehension, knowledge, and synthesis.

Learning Strategies: Describing, dramatizing, listing, observing, recording, and summarizing.

TEACHING STRATEGIES

1. Let students work with a friend or "friendly" partner. Ask them to interview each other to find out three skills and three special interests of the other person. Tell them to record this information on their activity sheets. (Every group has only one of these sheets. Each student adds his or her collected answers.)

2. After both students have finished, tell them to look at all the strengths, skills, and interests on their charts. Ask each group to discuss what a new person would be like with a combination of these attributes and characteristics.

3. Ask them to use their choice of filmstrip or CD-ROM story to find another "friend." Tell them to add that "friend's" skills and qualities to their list. Then direct them to take a digitized picture of both partners. They should fold their picture exactly in half and cut the two halves. Ask them to choose the two halves that go best and glue them together on a bristol board background.

4. To complete the chart on their activity sheets, they should write a co-operative description about their new "friend" using as many qualities combined on their charts as they can.

5. Encourage students to create a play about a fun time with their new friend.

I'm a Robot, Too!

Name_____

1.   Listen to some music.

2.   Be a robot. Move to the music.

3.   List jobs robots could do.

_____

_____

_____

4.   Pretend you are a robot doing a job.
     Think about how you move.

5.   Act out for the class a robot doing a
     job. Can they guess what your robot
     is doing?

How My Robot Moves	
arms	
legs	
head	

Title: **I'm a Robot, Too!**

Theme: **Inventions**

Subject: **Fine Art**

Materials Needed: Electronic or robot-type music (for example, "I am a Computer Man").

Learning Outcomes:
• Demonstrate awareness of body and movement, including direction, speed, level.
• Create a presentation based on music and movement.

Inquiry/Thinking Skills: Application, comprehension and synthesis.

Learning Strategies: Dramatizing, exploring, moving creatively, and listening.

TEACHING STRATEGIES

1. Before students begin this activity, invite them to explore ways of moving. They should think about speed, direction, level, body awareness, etc.

2. While seated, the students should listen to the robot music (for example, electronic music). Elicit what it makes them think of and why. Discuss types of movements that the music suggests. Talk about the different kinds of robots. Encourage them to relate the music to robot movement.

3. Tell students to pretend they are robots while they move to the music. Allow time for creative exploration of movement to the music. Provide praise for original and creative ideas, as well as encouragement to those who are more reluctant or shy. Introduce the concept of scenarios for variety. For example, the robot's battery runs down, the robot bumps into a wall, one part breaks down, there is a power serge (extra energy), and so on. Encourage students to brainstorm jobs robots might be able to do. Ask them (or help them) to write a list of likely jobs robots might do on their activity sheets.

4. After students have created their movements, ask them to present them to others. Shy children might feel more comfortable and produce better results if they perform in front of a few students only, rather than before the whole class. Challenge the audience to guess the robot's job.

Looking at Machines

Name_____

1. Find a machine in your classroom.

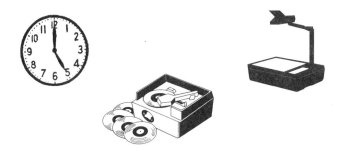 

2. Put on your inventor's glasses. Look at the machine closely.

3. Think of a new use for the machine. Give your new machine a name.

_____

4. Explain to a friend what your machine does.

Title: **Looking at Machines**

Theme: **Inventions**

Subject: **Social Studies**

Materials Needed: Various machines and tools found in and around the class and home (see activity sheet for examples), a pair of glasses to use as "inventor's" glasses (safety glasses, 3-D glasses, etc.).

Learning Outcomes: • Be able to compare and evaluate the design of everyday items.

Inquiry/Thinking Skills: Comprehension and synthesis.

Learning Strategies: Inventing, observing, and renaming.

TEACHING STRATEGIES

1. Brainstorm with students the various household and school machines that we use. Encourage them to understand that machines are supposed to make our lives easier. Have students explain the purpose of some of the machines.

2. Ask students to put on their "inventor's" glasses and look at one of the machines. Explain to students that the glasses "are to help you 'see' the machine differently." Suggest a new use for the machine. (For example, a fan could become a bubble machine by using it to blow bubbles automatically.)

3. Tell students to look at school and home for machines that could be used in a way that they were not intended. Ensure that students understand that **they are not to use them** in this unintended way.

SOMETHING TO THINK ABOUT

▶ Ask students: "How would you do everyday tasks without machines?" (For example, laundry and dishes would be done by hand, pencils would be sharpened with a knife, etc.).

Lost Dog!

Name_____

1. Make a Lost Dog poster. Plan your poster first:

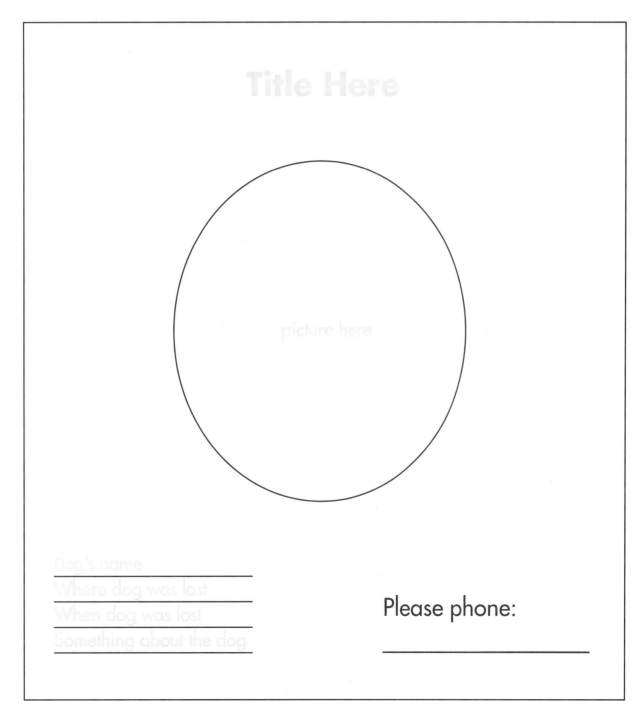

Title Here

picture here

Dog's name _____
Where dog was lost
_____
When dog was lost
_____
Something about the dog
_____

Please phone:

_____

Title:	**Lost Dog!**
Theme:	**Pets**
Subject:	**Fine Art**

Materials Needed: Tape recorder, filmstrip projector (a combined unit known as a Dukane projector would be more appropriate), tape and filmstrip story about a dog where there is a problem that is resolved in the story (for example, *Clifford the Big Red Dog* by Norman Bridwell), computer, primary publishing software.

Learning Outcomes:
• Use a range of media texts for entertainment and information.
• Experiment with the use of material from other media to enhance their writing.

Inquiry/Thinking Skills: Application, comprehension, and synthesis.

Learning Strategies: Designing and listening.

TEACHING STRATEGIES

1. Have students listen to and watch a story about a dog. Discuss the problem that emerged and was resolved in the story. Relate solving this problem to strategies that students would use to recover a lost pet dog.

2. Direct the discussion to a lost pet poster. Ask students to list the elements that would be needed on such a poster. (Refer them to the model on their activity sheets.)

3. Challenge students to create a Lost Dog Poster using an appropriate computer graphics program. Direct students to first plan their poster on their activity sheets.

4. Encourage students to evaluate these posters using the criteria previously established by the class.

SOMETHING TO THINK ABOUT

▶ Students could try to create a similar poster from the perspective of the dog: a Lost Owner Poster.

Making Greeting Cards

Name_____

1. What is the special occasion? _____

2. Who is sending the card?_____

3. Who is receiving the card? _____

4. What will go on the outside of my card?

   _____

   _____

5. What will be printed inside my card?

   _____

   _____

6. Here is a drawing to show what my card will look like.

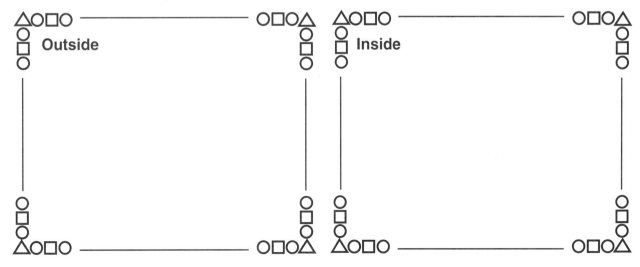

Title: **Making Greeting Cards**

Theme: **Celebrations**

Subject: **Fine Art**

Materials Needed: Computer, digital or Polaroid camera, primary graphics software.

Learning Outcomes:
- Produce messages combining a photographic image and print.
- Use specific poetry forms.

Inquiry/Thinking Skills: Comprehension and synthesis.

Learning Strategies: Composing, designing, and writing.

TEACHING STRATEGIES

1. Share a number of greeting cards from the students' own collections and note the three main elements: an outside illustration, an outside and/or inside greeting. Discuss with them the attributes of each: simple lettering, brevity, friendliness, etc.

2. Direct students to design and make their own greeting cards. They could be used for birthdays or other special occasions.

3. Ask students to suggest appropriate photographic images for the cards' illustrations. (A birthday card might include an image of the greeter or the birthday recipient, a get-well wish to a classmate could include images of students, etc.) Have them plan how the picture might be composed with a 35 mm, Polaroid or video camera. (Model the correct use of the photographic equipment for the students.)

4. Tell the students to work in pairs or small groups to complete their photographs. Ask them to plan their cards on their worksheets and then produce a final copy using art materials and the computer, integrating their photographs.

SOMETHING TO THINK ABOUT

▶ Challenge students to use a particular form of poetry for their greeting card verse. Here are some forms that might be suitable: cinquain, limerick, acrostic, free verse.

Map Making

Name_____

1. Fill in the compass:

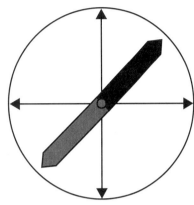

N = North
S = South
E = East
W = West

2. Make a map of your room.

Title: **Map Making**

Theme: **Geography**

Subject: **Social Studies**

Materials Needed: Examples of compasses, writing and drawing materials, computer, primary graphics program.

Learning Outcomes:
• Investigate relationships between the real and abstract world.
• Follow verbal instructions.

Inquiry/Thinking Skills: Analysis, comprehension, knowledge, and synthesis.

Learning Strategies: Creating, mapping, and recording.

TEACHING STRATEGIES

1. Discuss with students the directions of a compass: north, south, east, and west. Have them examine various compasses, using them as models to complete the compass on the activity sheets.

2. As a class group, look around the library and find the directions **N**orth, **S**outh, **E**ast, and **W**est. Have students align a piece of paper in the same direction as the library. Ask them to find **N**orth and put it on the map. Tell them to do the same for each of the cardinal points.

3. Say to students: "Imagine you are on the ceiling looking down. Still looking north, draw what you see." Ask them to look south and draw what they see. Repeat for east and west. Challenge them to fill in the middle of the map as they would see it from the ceiling, indicating all furniture.

4. Work with students to list all they see in the library. Encourage them to label their library map from the list.

5. Direct them to make a map of their bedroom on their activity sheets in the same way. Help them use a primary paint program to create a computer version of their bedroom map. Display the printouts.

More Tools

Name_____

1. Use a CD-ROM encyclopedia to find these pictures.

circular saw, hacksaw, plane, nail, crosscut saw, nuts and bolts

Circular Saw	Hacksaw
Plane	Crosscut Saw
Nail	Nuts and Bolts

IRWIN
Q
QUICK START MASTERS

Title: **More Tools**

Theme: **Tools**

Subject: **Social Studies**

Materials Needed: CD-ROM encyclopedia, glue, scissors, assorted tools.

Learning Outcomes:
- Use a wide range of processes, techniques, tools, and materials to gather information, solve problems, create and evaluate products, and communicate results.

Inquiry/Thinking Skills: Analysis, evaluation, and synthesis.

Learning Strategies: Classifying, creating, and evaluating.

TEACHING STRATEGIES

1. Ask students to use a CD-ROM encyclopedia to find pictures of and information on these common tools: circular saw, hacksaw, plane, nail, crosscut saw, nuts and bolts. (Alternatively, each group finds, prints out a picture, and draws *one* of the above tools. When all groups have finished, there will be one complete activity sheet.) Ask students to draw these tools on their activity sheets. They also can paste the printout of each tool onto their sheets.

2. If needed, help some students search the CD-ROM for the tools, then let these students teach others these search methods.

3. Ask students (or groups) to identify what occupations use each tool. (There can be more than one occupation that uses a tool.)

4. Invite students to draw a picture that represents one of the above occupations.

SOMETHING TO THINK ABOUT

▶ Plan a visit to a Design and Technology class to see how each tool is used. Record on videotape the special uses of each tool.

▶ Using some of the tools, in partnership with a Middle School student or a volunteer, encourage students to make something that works. Ask them to tell about what they have learned.

Movie Monsters

Name_____

1. Draw a picture of a monster you would like to see in a movie.

2. Make a model of your monster out of plasticene. With your group, make a setting or place for your monsters.

3. Plan out a story for your monsters.

4. Use your monster models to act out the story.

5. Videotape your story. Add sound effects or words to help tell your story. Play your videotape for the class.

Title:	**Movie Monsters**	
Theme:	**Monsters**	
Subject:	**Fine Art**	

Materials Needed: Coloured paper, glue, other art supplies, plasticene, scissors, tripod, VCR, video camera.

Learning Outcomes: • Use technology to produce a short animation.

Inquiry/Thinking Skills: Application and synthesis.

Learning Strategies: Constructing and sequencing.

TEACHING STRATEGIES

1. Discuss with the class the possible attributes and appearance of monsters. Develop a descriptive theme vocabulary.

2. Ask students to draw their own monsters. Using plasticene, have students construct three-dimensional representations of the monsters.

3. In groups, ask students to design and construct a setting for their monsters, using an open box and coloured paper. Have each group develop a brief story or *scenario* involving their monsters in this setting.

4. Use the principles of stop-motion animation to act out the scenario and videotape:
a) Set the video camera on a tripod, close enough to the scene to fill the frame.
b) Shoot at least five seconds of video without moving the plasticene monsters.
c) Move each figure a limited amount and shoot a very brief time (one second or less).
d) Repeat this action for each movement until the entire scenario is completed.
e) Add five seconds of non-action video at the end.

5. Play the completed animation film for the group.

SOMETHING TO THINK ABOUT

▶ Ask students to create narration, dialogue, and sound effects for their animated films by using an audio-dubbing VCR.

My New Classroom

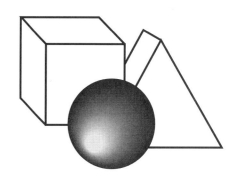

Name_____

1. Draw a plan for your new classroom:

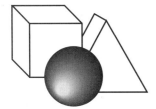

Title: **My New Classroom**

Theme: **Shapes**

Subject: **Fine Art**

Materials Needed: Construction set such as Lego, paper, crayons, real blueprint (optional).

Learning Outcomes: • Demonstrate knowledge of how to build a structure.

Inquiry/Thinking Skills: Application, comprehension, and synthesis.

Learning Strategies: Constructing, creating, and organizing.

TEACHING STRATEGIES

1. Brainstorm with students the kinds of subjects that are learned in school (music, art, physical education, writing, etc.). Have them identify the areas in the classroom that they like best and tell why they like them (painting at the paint centre, for example).

2. Ask students to tell about areas in the rest of the school that they like and why they like them. Encourage them to focus on things that make them learn, not just provide fun.

3. Lead them in brainstorming on what they would like in the classroom of their dreams. Tell them they will build these elements using the construction set.

4. Direct them to first plan their classroom by drawing a map-like view on their activity sheets. Then give students a piece of construction paper on which to build their ideal classroom. When they are done, they can use the model as a guide to make a blueprint of their work by tracing around the objects that they have designed. This will help students make the connection between a 3-D model and a map.

SOMETHING TO THINK ABOUT

▶ You may show students what a real blueprint looks like and choose to have them draw on blue paper using white chalk to make the drawings look like blueprints.

Name That Sound!

Name_____

1.   Think about all the sounds cars, airplanes, and trains make.

2.   Tape some of them.

3.   Play Name That Sound! Play your tape for your friends. See if they can name that sound.

4.   Make up a story about where you will go. Use your tape to make the sounds.

Title: **Name That Sound!**

Theme: **Transportation**

Subject: **Social Studies**

Materials Needed: Tape recorder, primary word-processing software.

Learning Outcomes:
• Use a variety of methods to gather, display, and communicate information.
• Apply oral language across the curriculum.
• Listen for enjoyment and to acquire information.

Inquiry/Thinking Skills: Application, knowledge, and synthesis.

Learning Strategies: Creating a story/poem, editing the tape, manipulating a tape recorder, and presenting to a group.

TEACHING STRATEGIES

1. Help students to become familiar with the operation of the tape recorder for recording sound. Some prior practice would help to ensure success during actual recording.

2. Stress the importance of being safe outdoors. Discuss how students should never go too close to traffic, railway tracks, and other systems of transportation.

3. Encourage students to think of resources for gathering different transportation sounds. Many commercials and movies contain a variety of sounds. Video games also use sound effects to enhance their programs.

4. Ask students to make up a travel story or poem that would benefit from using sound effects.

5. In order to get the sound effects in the right order for their story or poem, it might be necessary for students to retape the sounds, altering the order in which they are heard. Help them write their story or poem (using a word-processing program if suitable).

6. Encourage them to read or tell their story or poem (with sound effects) to the class.

Ocean Life

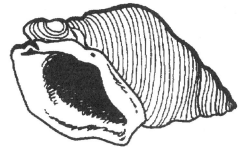

Name_____

1. Find out about life in the ocean. What animals live there?

2. Use a CD-ROM and books about the ocean to find out about ocean life.

3. Make a picture book about the ocean. Here are some ideas:

alphabet book   story book   school book

4. Use a computer to make pictures. Print out pictures from the CD-ROM.

Author Page

5. Make an author page about you.
Put your picture on the page.

6. Share your book with a friend.

Title:	**Ocean Life**
Theme:	**Oceans**
Subject:	**Social Studies**

Materials Needed: CD-ROM encyclopedia, print resources on the ocean, paper, pencil, pencil crayons.

Learning Outcomes: • Select an appropriate medium and produce simple text for specific purposes and audiences.

Inquiry/Thinking Skills: Knowledge and synthesis.

Learning Strategies: Creating, locating, researching, and writing.

TEACHING STRATEGIES

1. Tell students that they are going to explore oceans and ocean life. Present to them a collection of ocean resource material, including a CD-ROM encyclopedia.

2. Ask them to search in the CD-ROM resource for **Ocean Life** or **Sea Animals**.

3. Help them to gather information about ocean animals. (Have them select five to ten sea creatures or plants.)

4. Discuss with students the type of picture books they like to read: alphabet books, story books, information books, school texts.

5. Ask them to make a picture book about the ocean. (They can choose one of the formats illustrated on their activity sheets or do one of their own.)

6. Encourage them to record their information in a simple, clear way (a few sentences for sharing with other primary students). For their pictures or illustrations, they can print out screens from the CD-ROM encyclopedia, cut pictures from magazines, or do their own.

7. These books can be shared with other students, as well as included in the library.

School Helpers

Name_____

1. Who works at your school?

_____   _____

_____   _____

_____   _____

_____   _____

2. Draw a picture of your helper.

IRWIN
Q
QUICK START
MASTERS

Jobs to Do
1. Clean my room
2. Wash the dishes
3. Rake the lawn

Title: **School Helpers**

Theme: **Jobs**

Subject: **Social Studies**

Materials Needed: Tape recorder, overhead projector and acetates, computer, award maker (or greeting card) software.

Learning Outcomes:
- Use technology in creative activities.
- Use technology (tape recorder, overhead projector) to gather and communicate information.
- Work constructively with others.
- Demonstrate awareness of the contributions of various people to the school community.

Inquiry/Thinking Skills: Application, comprehension, and evaluation.

Learning Strategies: Interviewing, recalling, using a tape recorder, using publishing software, and presenting.

TEACHING STRATEGIES

1. With the class, list all the people who work at the school. Tell students to record the list on their activity sheets.

2. Discuss what jobs the people do and why it is important to have these helpers.

3. Tell the class they are going to be interviewing some of the helpers and will be taping the questions and answers. Elicit from students what questions they think would be good to ask. (What is your name? What do you do in your job?) Have students practise interviewing and tape-recording techniques with others in the class prior to their actual interviews. (Remind them about the need for politeness.) Students should work in pairs so that one can operate the tape recorder while the other conducts the interview. Organize which students will interview which school helpers, so the helpers do not become overwhelmed with interviews.

4. Tell students to draw a picture of one of these helpers on their activity sheets. Encourage them to use markers to illustrate the helpers on overhead acetates.

5. Have some students make thank-you certificates for the helpers.

6. Have a multi-media presentation of the pictures and taped interviews and invite the helpers if possible.

Sharing Apples

Name_____

1. Put the recipe steps in order:

___   Add the water

___   Sprinkle with cinnamon.

___   Wash the apples.

___   Cook and stir the apples.

___   Cut up the apples.

___   Eat it up!

___   Cool the applesauce.

___   Making Applesauce

___   Peel the apples.

___   Add the sugar.

2.   The Taste Test:

Not Bad																		
Good																		
Great!																		

Title: **Sharing Apples**

Theme: **Food**

Subject: **Social Studies**

Materials Needed: Microwave oven and/or crock pot, cooking utensils, apples.

Learning Outcomes: • Use social skills in small-group work.
                             • Describe the benefit of sharing.
                             • Sequence steps.

Inquiry/Thinking Skills: Application, comprehension, and evaluation.

Learning Strategies: Organizing and problem solving.

TEACHING STRATEGIES

1. Present the students with the following problem: "We have 13 apples for recess snack and 21 students. How are we going to share the apples?" (*Any numbers may be used as long as the students cannot solve the problem mathematically.*)

2. Encourage students to brainstorm as many possible solutions as possible. Eliminate the solutions that will obviously not work and discuss the merits of the remaining solutions.

3. Discuss why *applesauce* is the best solution for this problem.

4. Direct students to go to the library to locate recipes for applesauce or have a recipe on hand for immediate use.

5. With the class, read the recipe and decide on the jobs that need to be done. Include in the discussion hygiene and safety factors that should be considered when preparing food. Invite students to prepare the recipe and taste/share the results.

6. Model for students how to make a simple bar graph or make a class taste graph on the board similar to the one on their activity sheets. Have students complete the activity sheet and The Taste Test graph.

Sing a Song

Name_____

1. What songs do you know?

Row, Row, Row Your Boat   **Three Blind Mice**   **Twinkle, Twinkle Little Star**   **The Bear Went over the Mountain**   **London Bridge Is Falling Down**

2. Make up a song about travelling.

3. Use a computer to make music.

4. Now sing along to the music!

Title: **Sing a Song**

Theme: **Transportation**

Subject: **Fine Art**

Materials Needed: Computer, music-maker software, tape recorder and microphone, writing materials (or word-processing program).

Learning Outcomes:
- Use a variety of materials to create and perform works of art.
- Use symbols to represent sounds.

Inquiry/Thinking Skills: Application, knowledge, and synthesis.

Learning Strategies: Manipulating music-maker software, recording on tape recorder, transposing sounds to notes, writing a poem.

TEACHING STRATEGIES

1. Have students brainstorm the names of various simple songs. Write the titles on the blackboard. You might even want to sing a few lines, too! Some possible titles are: Row, Row, Row Your Boat; Three Blind Mice; Twinkle, Twinkle Little Star; London Bridge Is Falling Down; Frère Jacques.

2. Work with the class to create co-operatively a *travelling* song. Then ask students to work in pairs or groups to make their own. Here is a sample song (to the tune of Row, Row, Row Your Boat):
   Drive, drive, drive the car
   Slowly down the street.
   Stop the car and out we jump.
   Now wasn't that a treat!

3. Demonstrate music-maker software to students. Input the notes from the song that the class created. It would be helpful for students to sing the song as you record in order to tone-match the correct notes.

4. Let each group record their song on audio tape (with the computer playing the tune).

SOMETHING TO THINK ABOUT

▶ Explore the music-maker software with students. See what rhythm beats and/or accompaniment can be added to their songs.

Smile!

Name_____

1. Cut out a cardboard camera like this:

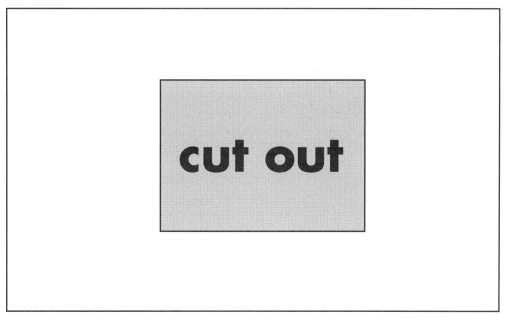

2. Take a picture of your friend with the cardboard camera.

3. Ask your friend to show different feelings:

happy   **sad**   **mad**   **afraid**

Title: **Smile!**

Theme: **Feelings**

Subject: **Fine Art**

Materials Needed: Polaroid cameras, cardboard camera "viewfinders."

Learning Outcomes:
• Understand the intended message of a photograph.
• Plan and construct a visual (photographic) message.

Inquiry/Thinking Skills: Analysis, application, and evaluation.

Learning Strategies: Constructing, describing, and role-playing.

TEACHING STRATEGIES

1. Ask students to think about ways photographs differ from "real life." Here are some possible responses: pictures do not move; there is no sound; pictures are one moment in time, they do not change; pictures show only *some* things, much is left out.

2. Use cardboard frames to simulate a camera viewfinder. (See activity sheet.) Have them experiment in framing a subject by moving the picture frame nearer and farther from the eye.

3. Ask them to take pictures of each other, using the cardboard frames.

4. Let students reflect on the photographer's usual instruction to *smile*. What other feelings can we express in a photograph? You might use a series of magazine photographs and/or tableaux to illustrate the use of facial and body language in expressing emotion.

5. Encourage them to use the cardboard cameras to take pictures of one another, displaying a number of different emotions (using different expressions and body language).

6. Instruct students in the care and handling of the Polaroid camera. Working in pairs or small groups, have them photograph each other, filling the frame with the subject and illustrating a particular, specified emotion.

7. Display the finished photographs in groups illustrating the various emotions portrayed. Ask students to talk about how successful the photographs were in achieving their intent.

Talking with Others

Name_____

1. Talking with people:

2. Telling people things:

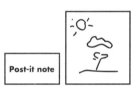   

3. Make a booklet like this:

Ways to Tell Things Without Talking

FRONT

| I can draw a picture. |
| I can use a post-it note. **Swimming 9 a.m.** |

BACK

| To tell about: going on a picnic |
| To tell about: remembering swiming |

Title:	**Talking with Others**
Theme:	**Communication**
Subject:	**Social Studies**

Materials Needed: Assortment of media devices: telephone, walkie-talkie, answering machine, cell phone, intercom, radio, television, newspaper, magazines, signs, CDs, tapes, pictures of skywriting, etc.

Learning Outcomes:
• Describe how certain technologies affect their lives.
• Use some types of technology in creative activities.
• Work constructively with others on projects.
• Use various types of information technology for a variety of purposes.

Inquiry/Thinking Skills: Application, comprehension, knowledge, and synthesis.

Learning Strategies: Creating a collage, exploring media devices, recalling, seriating, recording, and role-playing.

TEACHING STRATEGIES

1. With students, brainstorm ways that they talk to other people. Put the names of these ways on flashcards, with a picture clue for each one. Encourage them to circle the matching illustration on their activity sheets. Introduce the appropriate media devices as they are mentioned (or give clues to elicit responses that call for these devices). Have individual students seriate the cards from the most commonly used to the least.

2. Provide opportunities for the students to try out these devices. Some discussion about correct manners/etiquette might be appropriate at this time.

3. Brainstorm ways that we tell people things without actually talking. Tell students to circle the matching illustrations. Discuss when they might use these ways *instead* of talking and have them give examples.

4. Make mini-books to record this information. (See activity sheet for a model.)

5. Direct students to role-play, performing a task or miming an event where no talking is involved. Videotape the skits and invite others to guess what the task/event is about. (Note: You might have to demonstrate, initially, in order for them to get the idea.)

class • group • pairs • individuals

Telephone Calls

Name_____

1. Type of call:

   ❑   emergency

   ❑   parent at work

   ❑   grandma, uncle, etc.

   ❑   friend

   ❑   unknown caller

2. Information for telephone call:

   a)_____

   b)_____

   c)_____

   d)_____

   e)_____

   Caller:_____

   Receiver:_____

IRWIN
QUICK START MASTERS

Title: **Telephone Calls**

Theme: **Tools**

Subject: **Social Studies**

Materials Needed: Disconnected telephones.

Learning Outcomes:
- Identify the telephone as a familiar technology used in the home and school.
- Describe ways in which the telephone has made daily life better or worse.
- Identify the consequences of decisions and actions in daily life.

Inquiry/Thinking Skills: Application, comprehension, and synthesis.

Learning Strategies: Demonstrating and problem-solving.

TEACHING STRATEGIES

1. Discuss with the class why the telephone is an important piece of equipment to have in the house or why some people may consider the telephone a nuisance. Brainstorm all the uses of a telephone.

2. Establish criteria for each type of telephone call a child can make and what information must be included.

3. With the help of the students, write role-play scenarios for the use of the telephone. Also include other scenarios the students did not help write. Divide the scenarios among groups. Using the activity sheet, have each group decide what type of telephone call the scenario asks for.

4. Tell each group to plan the information to be included in the telephone call. Encourage them to role-play two or three scenarios and present some of these to the class.

Tools We Use

Name_____

1. What do these tools do?

2. Make something that can carry things from one place to another. Draw your invention.

Title: **Tools We Use**

Theme: **Tools**

Subject: **Social Studies**

Materials Needed: Electronic and hand-held tools (see examples on activity sheet), wood pieces, nails, screw, sandpaper.

Learning Outcomes: • Use a wide range of processes, techniques, tools, and materials to solve problems, create and evaluate products, and communicate results.

Inquiry/Thinking Skills: Application, comprehension, and knowledge.

Learning Strategies: Brainstorming, creating, evaluating, and investigating.

TEACHING STRATEGIES

1. Discuss with students each of the tools pictured on their activity sheets. If possible, have each of these tools in the classroom. Demonstrate their use.

2. Tell students they are going to make something that can carry things from one place to another.

3. Brainstorm with students a list of possible vehicles that can transport objects. Ask students to decide where their creation will move (for example, from water to land).

4. Ask them to select pieces of wood that they think can be used to create this vehicle. Encourage students to first draw (plan) their vehicles on their activity sheets.

5. Let them discover how each piece of wood could fit together and/or move. (For example, if they use square blocks for the wheels, what changes need to be made to make them move?)

SOMETHING TO THINK ABOUT

▶ Working with a parent volunteer, help students create their vehicles using electric and electronic tools (or use Design and Technology classes if you have Middle School students nearby). Encourage students to paint and sand their vehicles. Have them demonstrate how the vehicles move.

Toy Groups

Name_____

1. These are the toys I like best:

Title:	**Toy Groups**	
Theme:	**Games**	
Subject:	**Social Studies**	

Materials Needed: Collection of toys that do something, Venn diagrams.

Learning Outcomes:
• Identify common objects.
• Sort and classify them using their own and established criteria.

Inquiry/Thinking Skills: Analysis, application, comprehension, evaluating, and synthesis.

Learning Strategies: Categorizing and comparing.

TEACHING STRATEGIES

1. Bring in toys from home that "do" something.

2. Divide students into groups of four and have them decide different ways to classify the toy collection. Invariably the comment will come up: "But this toy goes into three different groups."

3. Demonstrate how to use a Venn diagram to classify, categorize, and display this information. (For example, dolls = battery group, people/children group, and boys/girls group.)

4. Take a video of each group's final divisions and direct students to explain on the video why they categorized the toys as they did.

5. After students have watched each completed segment, ask them to observe and comment on the differences and categories used for classification.

Two Ways of Looking

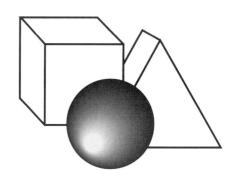

Name_____

1. Match the top to the side.

Top	**Side**

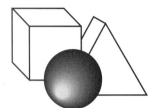

Title: **Two Ways of Looking**

Theme: **Shapes**

Subject: **Fine Art**

Materials Needed: Overhead projector, small 3-D objects to project (a pen, cup, etc.), 3-D objects that appear different from side and top view (see activity sheet), Polaroid or other camera, a construction set such as Lego.

Learning Outcomes: • Use appropriate models to investigate the natural and human-made worlds.

Inquiry/Thinking Skills: Application, comprehension, and knowledge.

Learning Strategies: Constructing, making a model, and observing.

TEACHING STRATEGIES

1. Discuss with students how an object can have a different shape when viewed from different points of view. (You can use the overhead to project views of different classroom objects.) Discuss what shapes they see, for example, the end of a pen is a circle while the length of the pen is like a rectangle).

2. Challenge them to complete their activity sheets, matching the *top* and *side* views of various classroom objects. (The first one has been done for them.)

3. Direct students to take a picture of an object that appears different from two points of view (or have them work from the real object). They should choose objects that are more complex than a pen, such as a doll house, a desk, a chair, etc. Ask them to make a model of the object using a construction set based on the two different points of view.

4. The photos and the models can be displayed together so that students can guess what model goes with which picture, or the class can guess using the models and trying to find the real object in the classroom.

Work Tools

Jobs to Do
1. Clean my room
2. Wash the dishes
3. Rake the lawn

Name_____

1. I went to visit the _____

2. The _____ works in the _____

3. My question: _____

   _____

4. The answer: _____

Tools and Work

Tool	Manual Energy	Other Energy
Computer		electricity
3-hole-punch	yes	
Lawn mower		gasoline
Screw driver	yes	
Drill		electricity
Refrigerator		electricity

IRWIN
Q
QUICK START
MASTERS

Jobs to Do
1. Clean my room
2. Wash the dishes
3. Rake the lawn

Title: **Work Tools**

Theme: **Jobs**

Subject: **Social Studies**

Materials Needed: Primary word-processing software, computer, school and outside resource people.

Learning Outcomes:
• Identify and describe the kinds of tools used by people in their work.
• Differentiate among tools as to the energy used to make them work.

Inquiry/Thinking Skills: Analysis and knowledge.

Learning Strategies: Observing and recording.

TEACHING STRATEGIES

1. Divide students into groups.

2. Plan for each group to visit workers within the school (caretaker, nurse, secretary, principal, daycare worker, etc.) to find out what tools are used to make their work easier.

3. Before going on the visit, have students brainstorm what they expect to see and the type of energy source the tools may use. Have each group prepare a list of questions they wish to ask.

4. As a group or individually, ask students to fill out their activity sheets at each visit. Create for students in a word-processing program a chart similar to the one on the activity sheet (Tools and Work). Tell each group to complete and print out their chart. (You might want to complete a sample chart on an overhead projector that students can do on their activity sheets.)

5. Guest visitors can be included from among the parents (electrician, hairdresser, florist, etc.). As well, guests might also bring some of the tools they use with them.

SOMETHING TO THINK ABOUT

▶ If your school is in an area that is easily accessible to businesses, you could arrange for the students to visit some to complete a similar activity. This out-of-school visit may give the students examples of more sophisticated tools and energy sources.